REGIONAL W

THE PEAK DISTRICT

Paul Sterry

DIAL
HOUSE

First published 1995

ISBN 0 7110 2293 3

© Paul Sterry 1995

Published by Dial House

an imprint of Ian Allan Ltd, Terminal House, Station Approach, Shepperton, Surrey TW17 8AS;
and printed by Ian Allan Printing Ltd, Coombelands House, Coombelands Lane, Addlestone, Weybridge, Surrey KT15 1HY.

Contents

INTRODUCTION

*Dominating north-west Derbyshire
in the heart of England, few areas
of untamed Britain are so easily accessible
to so many people as the Peak District.
Huge conurbations are dotted around the region's
periphery, making day trips an easy option
for hundreds of thousands of potential visitors.*

Because of man's long association with the Peak District,
not least through modern-day tourism, the area can hardly
be described as wilderness Britain any longer. Nevertheless,
there is ample scope for those seeking peace and quiet, and the
variety of wildlife and terrain is truly remarkable considering
the comparatively small area defined as the Peak District.

Following the 1949 National Parks Act, the Peak District became
the first region in England and Wales to be designated a National
Park; the actual designation occurred in 1950, and its official name
became the Peak National Park. This enshrinement in law reflected
the importance of the region as part of the national heritage.

One reason for conferring National Park status on the Peak
District was to preserve the integrity of the landscape for future
generations. This was not to be to the exclusion of a variety of
economic factors, however; for example, a range of mining
activities still continues. Wildlife conservation in the strict sense
was not a fundamental reason for the establishment of the National
Park. Nevertheless, the protection of the landscape has obviously
benefited the natural history of the area and there is still a wealth
of plants and animals to be found and enjoyed.

The richness of the Peak District's wildlife heritage owes as much to
its geographical location as to the varied rock types that comprise
the region. Situated at the southern tip of the Pennines, many of
the plants and animals found here have their southernmost British
outposts in the Peak District, their main ranges lying in the uplands
of northern Britain. These species occur in addition to ones that
are widespread throughout southern and central England.

Lots of plants and animals are sensitive to soil chemistry:
with limestone outcrops and acid moors on rocks of millstone grit
in the region, a wide variety of tolerances are catered for.
Add all these factors together and it is not surprising that
birdwatchers and botanists alike enthuse about the region.

MAP OF THE PEAK DISTRICT

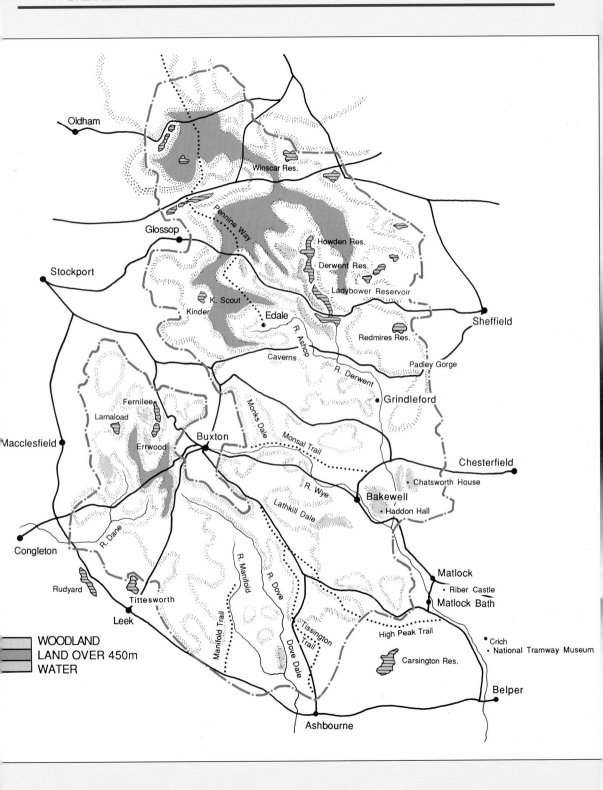

WOODLAND
LAND OVER 450m
WATER

Oldham
Winscar Res.
Glossop
Pennine Way
Stockport
Howden Res.
Derwent Res.
Ladybower Reservoir
K. Scout
Kinder
Edale
Sheffield
R. Ashop
Redmires Res.
Caverns
Padley Gorge
R. Derwent
Fernilee
Grindleford
Lamaload
Monks Dale
Errwood
Buxton
Monsal Trail
Macclesfield
Chesterfield
R. Wye
Chatsworth House
Lathkill Dale
Bakewell
R. Dane
Haddon Hall
Congleton
R. Manifold
R. Dove
Matlock
Rudyard
Riber Castle
Tittesworth
Matlock Bath
Manifold Trail
Tissington Trail
High Peak Trail
Crich
Leek
National Tramway Museum
Dove Dale
Carsington Res.
Belper
Ashbourne

The geology of the Peak District is complex. It is at the heart of the diversity of the region's vegetation and wildlife, with two rock types in particular exerting dominating and contrasting influences.

A large mass of limestone, known as the White Peak, dominates the south of the Park and is carved with radiating valleys around its flanks. Encompassing the limestone on its western, northern and eastern borders are coarse sandstone rocks, called millstone grit; this horseshoe-shaped upland region is known as the Dark Peak. While limestone and sandstone form the dominant extremes in soil type, areas of shale and, to a lesser extent, volcanic rocks also occur.

The underlying soil type undoubtedly has a profound influence on the vegetation in a particular area and this is clearly demonstrated here. In many areas, however, the influence of man over the centuries has also had an important role in modifying the vegetation.

So strong has this effect been that, in some places, the influence of man and environmental factors are inextricably linked.

An example of man's influence can be found by examining tree cover in the region. At one time, the natural vegetation of the Peak District would have been forest, with oaks probably predominating on acid soils and ash on lowland and limestone soils. Centuries of clearance have produced the vast moorland tracts we see today on acid soils and calcareous grassland in limestone regions.

Moorland

The acid soils overlying a bedrock of millstone grit are dominated by moorland vegetation. The moors stretch across large areas in the north and west of the park in particular, reaching their highest point — more than 600m — at Kinder Scout. Ling and bilberry are arguably the two most important plants of this habitat, with other heather species, sphagnum moss, cottongrass and bog asphodel, appearing in boggy areas. Moorland habitats have suffered more than most in the region from atmospheric pollution, including acidification — the result of industry nearby.

Woodland

While a few areas of native oak woodland, such as Ladybower Wood, persist in the region, ash is probably the dominant woodland-forming tree in the Peak District. Especially where it grows on lime-rich soils, a rich ground flora develops including species such as bluebells, ramsons, wood anemones and early purple orchids. Woodland birdlife is at its best in early spring when numbers of resident species are swollen by newly-arrived migrants.

Grassland

In the Peak District, as in most other regions in Britain, grassland has resulted after clearance of woodland from the land. In some areas, the wildlife interest is minimal due in part to the soil type and also to the continued influence of man through selective seeding and herbicides. In many limestone areas in the Peak District, however, rich calcareous grasslands have developed full of orchids and other unusual species; Lathkill Dale is a classic example. Man's continued influence is vital to the survival of these habitats: without grazing and cutting, scrub, and subsequently woodland, would develop.

Freshwater

Fast-flowing streams and stony rivers occur throughout the Peak District. Where disturbance and pollution are minimal, these aquatic habitats are home to a range of freshwater invertebrates; the health of the water is best demonstrated by the presence of fish and birds such as dippers and grey wagtails. To supply the water requirements of towns and cities around the Peak District, large reservoirs, such as Ladybower, have been built, whole valleys being submerged in the process.
While these do comparatively little to enhance the wildlife value of the region, they do provide an added and alternative dimension to the landscape.

The species described and illustrated in this book have been arranged in an order which follows the convention of relevant field guides to the region.

The selection is a mixture of the most characteristic and conspicuous members of the community together with specialities of the region. Species that are likely to arouse the curiosity of the visitor have also been included.

Where appropriate, the species' average length (L.) or height (H.) is given after the Latin name.
Other measurements which may help identification are incorporated into the text.

BIRDS

1 Mallard *Anas platyrhynchos* (L. 58cm)

Wildfowl are comparatively poorly represented in the Peak District and the mallard is one of the few species to be regularly encountered. Males can be identified by their grey-brown back and flanks, reddish-brown breast, greenish head and yellow bill. Females, by contrast, are mottled brown. In flight, both species show a blue patch on the trailing edge of the inner wing — this is known as the speculum. Mallards breed in small numbers in the Peak District. They are most easily seen on reservoirs within the region, sometimes in small flocks.

2 Teal *Anas crecca* (L. 36cm)

The teal is the smallest duck in Britain and hence also in the Peak District. When a good view is obtained, males have attractive plumage with a chestnut head, green stripe through the eye and greyish body feathering covered with fine vermiculations. The undertail is buffish-yellow and this sometimes shows up well from a distance. The female has a more subdued coloration and is mottled brown. This affords her excellent camouflage as she incubates her eggs among wetland and moorland vegetation. Teal are best looked for in the Peak District during the winter months when they haunt rush-fringed margins of reservoirs.

3 Tufted Duck *Aythya fuligula* (L. 43cm)

Between the months of October and March is the best time of year to see tufted ducks in the Peak District. These distinctive diving ducks favour open water on large reservoirs but will sometimes congregate in sheltered bays if the weather is severe. Male tufted ducks look black and white, although, in good light, a purple sheen can be seen on the dark feathering. As their name suggests, there is a prominent crest on the back of the head. Female tufted ducks have brownish plumage and a suggestion of a crest; sometimes a pale patch at the base of the bill is visible.

4 Kestrel *Falco tinnunculus* (L. 33cm)

Throughout the Peak District, the most likely bird of prey to be seen is the kestrel. Although it will take a variety of prey, it specialises in feeding on small mammals such as voles. These it locates primarily by hovering high above the ground, scanning with its powerful vision for the slightest movement. They also perch on roadside wires. Seen from above, the male kestrel has a chestnut back, black wingtips, blue-grey head and a blue-grey tail with a black terminal band. Females are a more uniform brown and have streaked underparts.

5 Merlin *Falco columbarius* (L. 27cm)

The merlin is Britain's smallest bird of prey. It is also one of the scarcest, although small numbers spend the summer months within the Peak District and a few are seen during the winter. Heather moorland is the preferred habitat of the merlin and it is often seen flying low over the ground in pursuit of a meadow pipit or other small bird; it occasionally perches on isolated posts as lookouts. Male merlins have steely grey upperparts and streaked, brown underparts. Females are slightly larger than males with brown upperparts and pale, streaked underparts.

6 Sparrowhawk *Accipiter nisus* (L. 30-37cm)

Scan the skies over areas of woodland in spring and you may be lucky enough to see a male sparrowhawk circling and displaying. Males are considerably smaller than females and have blue-grey upperparts and pale underparts that are barred and flushed with orange. Females have grey-brown upperparts and pale, barred underparts. Sparrowhawks feed on birds caught on the wing and their main hunting strategy is surprise. They characteristically fly along a hedgerow below bush height and then suddenly wheel over to the other side to catch a chaffinch unawares. Sudden attacks through woodland clearings are also common.

7 **Red Grouse** *Lagopus lagopus scoticus* (L. 38cm)
If any bird is characteristic of moorland in Britain, then it is the
red grouse. Heather-covered slopes offer the best chances of
seeing this cryptically marked gamebird whose distinctive 'go-
back, go-back, go-back' call is a familiar sound to hill walkers.
Although numbers have declined in recent years, at least
partly due to human disturbance, the red grouse is still fairly
common in the Peak District. Males have reddish-brown
plumage and a prominent red wattle over the eye; females are
more grey-brown in colour which affords them excellent
camouflage when incubating eggs among the heather clumps.

8 **Black Grouse** *Tetrao tetrix* (L. male 52cm female 42cm)
It usually takes perseverance and more than a little luck to
see a black grouse. Although large and distinctive, these
gamebirds are unobtrusive and keep to cover for most of the
day. The best time to see one is in the early morning from
late winter to early summer, when males display at traditional
sites called leks. Those that remain are likely to be on
undisturbed moorland and invariably close to the cover of a
conifer woodland. Males are mostly black with red wattles on
the head and a lyre-shaped tail which is spread during display
to reveal splayed, white undertail feathers. Females have
brownish plumage.

9 **Pheasant** *Phasianus colchicus*
(L. male 85cm female 62cm)
Although introduced into this country, the pheasant has
become well established over its stay of many centuries.
It is now a common sight in the Peak District, preferring areas
where copses and fields lie in close proximity to one another.
The loud, choking call of the pheasant is often heard, as is
the loud, explosive sound of wings and calls when a bird is
startled into flight. Males have gaudy orange-brown plumage
with an iridescent, bluish head and red wattle around the eye.
Females, on the other hand, have sandy-brown plumage.

10 **Moorhen** *Gallinula chloropus* (L. 33cm)
Marshy ground and the vegetated margins of reservoirs
provide ideal habitats for the moorhen in the Peak District.
Seen from a distance, the bird can look rather dark.
In good light, however, the upperparts are brownish and the
underparts are smoky-grey. Moorhens have a distinctive bill
and frontal shield which is bright red, the tip of the bill being
yellow. The legs are dull yellow with long toes and there is a
white streak along the flanks. They swim well and while doing
so flick their tails constantly to reveal the white undertail
feathers.

11 **Lapwing** *Vanellus vanellus* (L. 30cm)

The lapwing is still a fairly common sight in the Peak District, nesting as it does in fields and on areas of bare moorland. Although not unduly shy, however, they are excluded from more popular areas because of the inevitable disturbance by visitors. Seen on the ground, lapwings are distinctive waders that look black and white at a distance. They have a long crest and, in flight, have broad rounded wings. One of the most evocative sounds of open spaces is that of the lapwing, a curious, drawn-out screech. In the spring, they perform aerobatic displays and also frantically mob and dive-bomb intruders near the nest. If you experience this behaviour, move away quickly.

12 **Golden Plover** *Pluvialis apricaria* (L. 27cm)

The golden plover is one of the most characteristic moorland breeding birds in Britain. Despite human disturbance to its upland habitat, this alert bird still occurs in reasonable numbers between May and July. As its name suggests, the golden plover has golden-yellow scalloped margins to the feathers of the crown, nape and back. It is seen in the Peak District mainly during the breeding season, when a broad, white margin separates the upperparts from the black underparts which, in the male, run from the face to the belly; the female has a much reduced area of black.

13 Dunlin *Calidris alpina* (L. 18cm)

This small, long-billed wader is sometimes known as the 'plover's page' since it often nests in the vicinity of golden plovers. Whether this is a matter of choice, or simply because both require similar nesting habitats, is open to debate. During the breeding season, when they are encountered in the Peak District, dunlin have a reddish brown back and cap and pale underparts with a striking black belly. They have a delightful display song comprising grunts and trills, which, on still days, carries for a surprising distance over the moors.

14 Redshank *Tringa totanus* (L. 27cm)

Ever alert and quick to utter its shrill alarm call, the redshank is found in the Peak District mainly during the breeding season, from April to July. Damp moorland and boggy flushes with abundant rushes are favoured sites, although birds can sometimes be found feeding along the margins of reservoirs. As their name suggests, redshank have red legs, which are long and striking. The bill is long and straight, and has a red base. The plumage is mostly grey-brown and the underparts have bars and chevron markings in the summer months.

15 Common Sandpiper *Actitis hypoleucos* (L. 20cm)

Also known as 'willie wicket', the common sandpiper is a summer visitor to the Peak District, usually present from April to July. It is one of the few birds of the region that can be identified safely by habitat choice and behaviour alone. The common sandpiper is invariably found beside water, sometimes the stony margins of reservoirs, but more usually along fast-flowing streams. It feeds unobtrusively on waterside invertebrates and frequently stands on stones and boulders in the water, all the while bobbing up and down and pumping the tail and rear of its body up and down.

16 Curlew *Numenius arquata* (L. 55cm)

This large wader can be easily recognised by its size and the immensely long, downcurved bill, used for probing damp ground for invertebrates. The plumage is brownish, the feathers of the back having buffish, scalloped margins. Curlew are found in the Peak District from April to July, breeding in typical wader habitats including marshy fields and moorland. Although not especially numerous in the region, they make their presence known with the loud 'curlew' call and evocative song comprising call-like phrases combined with beautiful, bubbling notes.

LATHKILL DALE

Lathkill Dale is a beautiful limestone valley that is administered by English Nature as a nature reserve; access is via a public footpath that runs down the valley.

A stream parallels the course of the path and is flanked by woodlands of ash and sycamore. Steep scree slopes rise up on either side along parts of the route with calcareous grassland on the valley floor. A superb array of flowers can be found in early summer and these include Jacob's-ladder, a nationally rare plant that has its centre of distribution in the Peak District.

Upper: Mossy Saxifrage Saxifrage hypnoides

17 Snipe *Gallinago gallinago* (L. 25cm)

When seen in outline, the snipe is an unmistakable wader, mainly because of the incredibly long bill; this is used to probe soft, muddy ground for worms and other invertebrates and is employed rather in the manner of a sewing machine. At close range, the plumage is an intricate mixture of brown, black, buff and white which, combined, afford excellent camouflage if the bird remains motionless among the rushes. Snipe are usually confident of their disguise and as a rule flush only if disturbed at close range; they fly off steeply, uttering a loud, sneezing call.

18 Cuckoo *Cuculus canorus* (L. 33cm)

Although many people think of the cuckoo as a lowland bird, it is surprisingly widespread in moorland areas too, including the Peak District. The first birds arrive in late April and males immediately start uttering their diagnostic 'cuck-oo' calls; females, by contrast, give a bubbling call. Cuckoos are brood parasites, laying their eggs in the nests of smaller birds. In the Peak District, the favoured victim is the meadow pipit. Nearly full-grown, immature cuckoos, with brown, barred plumage, are sometimes seen on open moorland in July, still being fed by their diminutive foster parents.

19 Skylark *Alauda arvensis* (L. 18cm)

From early spring until late summer, the song of the skylark is a familiar sound in many parts of the Peak District. Usually delivered in flight, the incessant rich and warbling song sometimes continues for hours on end as the songster climbs ever higher and higher into the skies. When seen on the ground, skylarks are rather nondescript birds with brown upperparts and paler, slightly streaked underparts. Skylarks are found in areas of rough pasture and rush-covered moors. In the winter, most leave the region, moving to lower ground.

20 Meadow Pipit *Anthus pratensis* (L. 14cm)
The meadow pipit is a bird of the open moors, especially in areas where clumps of rushes and grasses are interspersed with more open areas of shorter grass. The bird itself is rather nondescript, having brown upperparts and paler, buffish underparts, the latter with pronounced dark streaking. Meadow pipits are seen mostly on the ground, where they prefer to run rather than hop. In the spring, however, males sometimes engage in a short song-flight, gradually descending to the ground as the song ends in a series of drawn-out 'see-see-see' notes.

21 Tree Pipit *Anthus trivialis* (L. 15cm)
Although superficially similar to the meadow pipit, the habits and habitat preferences of this species make it comparatively easy to identify. The tree pipit is a summer visitor to the Peak District and is found in wooded valleys with sunny glades. Its most distinctive feature is its voice. The song is a loud and repetitive series of notes ending in thin, drawn-out phrases; it is usually delivered in a song-flight where the bird parachutes to the ground on stiffly-held wings. A close view of a tree pipit reveals a cleaner appearance than the meadow pipit, with an orange wash on the breast.

22 Grey Wagtail *Motacilla cinerea* (L. 18cm)
Invariably found beside water, the presence of grey wagtails on a river or stream is a sign of a healthy watercourse. These delightful birds are found throughout the Peak District in suitable habitats and are commonly seen perched on mid-stream boulders, their tails continually being pumped up and down. As the name suggests, the grey wagtail has greyish upperparts and a lemon-yellow flush to the underparts, varying in intensity according to gender and time of year. In summer, the male has a black throat and prominent white moustachial and eye stripes. Females and winter males lack these contrasting patterns.

23 Jackdaw *Corvus monedula* (L. 33cm)

This small member of the crow family is a familiar sight in the vicinity of villages and farms in the Peak District, but is less so on open moorland. It has a distinctive, shuffling gait and at a distance can look uniformly dark. In good light, however, the feathers of the neck appear greyish and contrast with a dark cap; the eye is pale grey, an unusual colour among British birds. Jackdaws are often seen in small flocks. They are intelligent birds and soon learn to exploit a new food source, such as the leftovers from picnics, often near car parks.

24 Carrion Crow *Corvus corone* (L. 46cm)

Although not especially common in the Peak District, the carrion crow is, nevertheless, widespread. As a result of centuries of persecution, they are understandably wary of man and so occur mainly on the open moors and away from habitation. Carrion crows are sometimes confused with rooks. As a general rule, the latter are gregarious while crows are usually solitary in their habits. They also have a uniform black plumage and lack the long bill, with pale skin at the base, of the rook. As their name suggests, carrion crows scavenge and often feed on animal road casualties.

25 Dipper *Cinclus cinclus* (L. 18cm)

Stand beside almost any fast-flowing river or stream in the Peak District for long enough and you are highly likely to see a dipper. These engaging birds are habitually associated with water and are almost never seen away from it. The dipper is a dumpy bird, rather like an outsize wren in appearance. The upperparts are dark brown while underneath the throat and chest are white while the belly is dark chestnut. They are often seen perched on mid-stream boulders and feed by plunging into the torrent in search of aquatic insect larvae and other small prey.

26 Wren *Troglodytes troglodytes* (L. 10cm)

Despite the rigours of winter weather in the region, the diminutive wren is a common year-round resident in the Peak District. Most of the time, it forages secretively among the undergrowth in search of insects. When alarmed, however, it sometimes springs into view and utters its loud, rattling alarm call. In the spring, males sing a song that comprises elements of the alarm call with tuneful notes; considering the size of the bird, the song is amazingly loud. Wrens are found in all sorts of habitats in the region, even in surprisingly desolate areas of moorland.

27 **Dunnock** *Prunella modularis* (L. 15cm)
The dunnock's other name of 'hedge sparrow' gives a clue as to the preferred habitat of this bird. Hedgerows, and indeed almost any area of scrub or woodland with tangled undergrowth, provide the food and shelter sought by this somewhat retiring species. Dunnocks have rather subdued plumage, the upperparts being brown while the underparts are blue-grey. The bill is fine and used for feeding on insects and spiders. In the spring, male dunnocks shed their skulking natures and perch prominently to sing; the song is a rapid series of warbling notes.

28 **Willow Warbler** *Phylloscopus trochilus* (L. 11cm)
From the middle of April to the end of May, willow warblers can be heard singing in many parts of the Peak District. They favour a wide variety of habitats from woodland in the dales to patches of scrub, the only requirement being the presence of trees of some sort; willows are, as the bird's name suggests, often chosen but areas of birch or ash will do equally well. The willow warbler is a tiny migrant with greenish yellow plumage. Its song is a descending series of tuneful notes. This contrasts with that of the chiffchaff, a superficially identical bird, whose song resembles its name.

29 **Wood Warbler** *Phylloscopus sibilatrix* (L. 12cm)
The wood warbler is a summer visitor to Britain, present in the Peak District between May and August. As its name suggests, it favours woodland habitats, usually where the trees are mature and there is relatively little ground cover. At first glance, there is some similarity between this species and the willow warbler. The wood warbler does, however, have brighter plumage and a distinctive song. This has been likened to a coin spinning on a silver plate since it ends with a rapid, metallic trill. Wood warblers usually feed high in the tree canopy.

30 **Goldcrest** *Regulus regulus* (L. 9cm)
The goldcrest is the smallest bird found in the Peak District. Experienced birdwatchers can sometimes detect their presence first by the call, which is extremely high-pitched and beyond the hearing range of some people. Woodland is the favoured habitat of this species, birds foraging for insects among the leaves and twigs. They show a marked preference for conifers but can also be found in deciduous woodland, especially during the winter months when they associate with mixed flocks of small birds. Goldcrests have olive-brown upperparts, pale underparts and two pale wingbars. There is a yellow crown stripe on the head, bordered on each side by black.

31 **Wheatear** *Oenanthe oenanthe* (L. 14.5cm)
Early April often sees the return of one of the Peak District's most attractive summer visitors, the wheatear. This distinctive bird is often first noticed as it flies off, revealing its conspicuous white rump. When perched, males show a black mask through the eye, blue-grey upperparts, buffish underparts and black wings; the plumage of the female is a more sombre version of the male's. Wheatears can be found in open, grassy areas and moors, especially where stone walls are common. The birds often perch on these and sometimes even nest in crevices, although burrows in the ground are usually favoured.

32 **Pied Flycatcher** *Ficedula hypoleuca* (L. 13cm)
Wooded slopes with sunny clearings and mature trees offer the best chances of seeing a pied flycatcher. These distinctive birds arrive in May and, for the next couple of months, can be seen perched on prominent branches, scanning around for passing insects; these are caught in aerial forays. As their name suggests, male pied flycatchers are essentially black and white. In the female, the patterning is the same but the black is replaced by brown plumage. Pied flycatchers have a loud song and constantly flick their tails when perched.

Just to the east of Buxton, the Monsal Trail runs along the course of a former railway line.

A leaflet to accompany the walk can be obtained from National Park information centres in the area. Much of the trail passes through limestone country and an excellent range of grassland and scrub plants can be seen along the route; these include bloody crane's-bill as well as Jacob's-ladder. For a short stretch, the trail parallels the course of the River Wye.

Upper: Nottingham Catchfly Silene Nutans
Lower: Common Toadflax Linaria vulgaris

33 Robin *Erithacus rubecula* (L. 14cm)
Throughout the year, woods, gardens and hedgerows in the Peak District harbour robins. At least partly territorial even in winter, they are often keen to scrutinise intruders into their domain and can become quite bold and inquisitive in some areas. An adult robin is easy to recognise with the orange-red breast bordered with grey, white belly and brown upperparts. Juveniles are more uniformly brown but characteristically have pale buff streaks on the upperparts. Robins sing most actively in the spring and early summer but continue with a more subdued song during the winter months.

34 Redstart *Phoenicurus phoenicurus* (L. 14cm)
When seen well, a male redstart is easy to identify. The face and throat are black, the breast is orange-red and the crown and nape are grey except for the white forecrown. Females are more uniformly brown but both sexes share the characteristic red tail which is obvious in flight and quivered at rest. Redstarts are summer visitors to the Peak District, arriving in May and departing in August. They favour areas of open, mature woodland and nest in holes in trees; they will occasionally use a hole or crevice in a stone wall as an alternative.

35 Blackbird *Turdus merula* (L. 24cm)
The blackbird needs little introduction to most people, being widespread throughout the country. In the Peak District, as elsewhere, it is a common garden bird but it can also be found feeding on open areas of grassland away from habitation and on the edges of woods. The male blackbird is, as the name suggests, an all-black bird and a member of the thrush family; the bill is yellow as is the eye-ring; females and juveniles are brown. Blackbirds characteristically hop along the ground, pausing briefly to probe the soil for worms and other invertebrates.

36 Ring Ouzel *Turdus torquatus* (L. 24cm)
The ring ouzel is one of the speciality birds of the Peak District, seldom being found away from rocky outcrops on desolate moors. Although superficially blackbird-like, the male has a prominent white crescent on the breast which is immediately diagnostic. Females have rather washed-out, grey-brown plumage but share a suggestion of the male's white crescent. Ring ouzels are not year-round residents in the region but arrive in April and depart again in August. Just prior to departure, small flocks can sometimes be seen feeding on the berries of mountain ash.

37 Marsh Tit *Parus palustris* (L. 12cm)
Search among a roaming mixed flock of woodland birds in winter, and you are likely to find several marsh tits. This species is widespread and fairly common in the Peak District, preferring damp, wooded valley bottoms and wooded slopes. The marsh tit has grey-brown upperparts, pale underparts with a warm, buffish tinge, and a striking black cap and bib. It is an active feeder, searching among the twigs and buds for insects. It will occasionally also feed on the ground if a supply of seeds is located. Marsh tits nest in holes in trees.

38 Long-tailed Tit *Aegithalos caudatus* (L. 14cm)
When you see one long-tailed tit you are likely to see several. These delightful birds are invariably seen in flocks moving through the trees and bushes in search of insects. They fancifully resemble feather dusters with their fluffy, almost spherical bodies and long tails. Flocks on the move also call all the time, the most characteristic sound being a churring rattle. In the spring, long-tailed tits construct amazing spherical nests made almost entirely from lichens, mosses and spider's silk. They are usually built among brambles or thorny bushes, the spines providing a degree of protection from predators.

39 **Great Tit** *Parus major* (L. 14cm)
From early March onwards, great tits can be heard singing in woodlands throughout the Peak District. Sometimes written down as 'tea-cher, tea-cher, tea-cher', the song is loud and strident. There are numerous variations on the theme, however, and many unfamiliar bird songs in a woodland can be attributed to the great tit. Being so familiar, the attractive plumage of this species is often overlooked. The back is greenish, the underparts are yellow and the head is black with white cheeks; a black stripe continues down the centre of the breast from the throat and is wider in the male than the female.

40 **Blue Tit** *Parus caeruleus* (L. 12cm)
Like its close relative the great tit, the blue tit seldom excites birdwatchers, simply because it is so common and familiar. Take a close look, however, and you will discover a most attractive bird. The head has contrasting patterns of black and white, the underparts are yellow, the back is greenish and the wings and tail are blue. Blue tits can be found in woodlands and gardens in the Peak District and often visit bird feeders in the winter months. They nest in holes in trees, but readily take to nest boxes if provided for them.

41 **Nuthatch** *Sitta europaea* (L. 14cm)
The nuthatch is the only British bird that habitually climbs down trees as well as up them. It is a dumpy woodland bird which is fairly common in valleys in the Peak District. The upperparts are blue-grey while the underparts are a warm buffish-pink; there is a black stripe through the eye and the throat is white. Nuthatches nest in holes in trees. If the entrance hole is too large, they will plaster it up with mud to reduce the diameter. Nuthatches often feed high among the branches. If the trees are in leaf they can be difficult to spot, but listen for their loud, piping alarm call.

42 Chaffinch *Fringilla coelebs* (L. 15cm)

Woodlands, parks and gardens are all suitable habitats for the chaffinch, one of Britain's most widespread species and one which is fairly common in the Peak District. When seen in good light, the male is an attractive bird with pinkish underparts, a bluish crown, a brown back and a green rump. Females have sandy-buff plumage and both sexes have two white wingbars that are very noticeable in flight. Chaffinches feed mainly on seeds and, during the winter months, can be seen in small flocks feeding along hedgerows and on the woodland floor.

43 Linnet *Carduelis cannabina* (L. 13cm)

If you take a spring walk in the Peak District which encompasses hedgerows and patches of scrub, then you should hear the tinkling song of the linnet on your travels. At this time of year, males are attractive birds with a rosy breast, red on the crown, a chestnut back and white on the wings, rump and tail. Females, by contrast, have rather sombre, brown plumage. Outside the breeding season, linnets are often seen in small flocks. They feed mainly on seeds of wayside plants and, not surprisingly, favour areas where plants such as thistles thrive.

44 Yellowhammer *Emberiza citrinella* (L. 16cm)

The yellowhammer is a typical hedgerow bird in many of the more lush areas of the Peak District. In the spring, males perch on prominent branches and deliver their tuneful, rattling song, often rendered as 'a little bit of bread and no cheese'. As their name suggests, they have a considerable amount of yellow in the plumage. Males are brighter than females but both have a chestnut rump, best seen in flight. During the winter months, yellowhammers spend a considerable amount of time feeding on the ground in search of seeds.

45 Brown Hare *Lepus capensis*
During March and April, male brown hares
engage in almost comical bouts of combat and
fighting. One male may pursue another round
and round for several minutes or they may
even stand on their hind legs and box. Hares
are open-country animals, unlike their relative,
the rabbit. They have long ears, tipped with
black, and long legs with endurance to match.
When alarmed, they may take off at great
speed, but will also crouch low and thereby
blend in with their surroundings. Sadly, due to
persecution and disturbance, hares are
nowhere near as common as they used to be.

46 Mountain Hare *Lepus timidus*
While the brown hare is an animal of more
rural, lowland areas, its close relative, the
mountain hare, is a creature of the high moors;
their distributions seldom, if ever, overlap.
The mountain hare is more usually associated
with moors in northern Britain and here, in the
Peak District, finds an extremely southerly
outpost. It is slightly smaller than the brown
hare but is best distinguished by its coloration
which varies through the year. In the summer it
is blue-grey, while in winter the fur is moulted
to produce a white coat. This helps the animal
blend in when a blanket of snow covers the
terrain. Mild winters, however, mean that they
stand out rather than blend in with their
surroundings.

47 Rabbit *Oryctolagus cuniculus*
Introduced to this country centuries ago, the
rabbit is now established as a familiar part of
the British countryside; despite persecution, it
is very much a feature of lowland areas of the
Peak District. Unlike its relatives the brown
hare and mountain hare, the rabbit prefers
fields with hedgerows or areas of scrub.
It excavates extensive burrow networks and
spends much of the daytime underground.
Generally speaking, rabbits are reviled by
farmers and landowners for the damage they
do. They are, however, popular with visitors.

48 Wood Mouse *Apodemus sylvaticus*
Sit quietly for a while in an autumn woodland in
the Peak District and you will start to hear
scurrying sounds among the leaf litter. The
chances are that these may be made by wood
mice searching among the fallen leaves for
nuts and seeds. You can even do a bit of
detective work to confirm this: look for
hazelnuts and acorns with jagged-edged holes.
The wood mouse can reach a length of about
15cm, including the tail. The coat is warm
brown above but pale beneath. During the
summer months they are active mainly at
night, but in autumn and winter are
occasionally seen during the day.

47

48

MONK'S DALE

Most of the plants that are associated with limestone grassland can be found in abundance at Monk's Dale.

A nature reserve, administered by English Nature, the site comprises not only grassland but areas of woodland and limestone scree too. Visitors must stick to public rights of way.

Lower: Herb Paris Paris quadrifolia

49 Short-tailed Vole *Microtus agrestis*
Grassland of all sorts, so long as it is undisturbed and not cultivated, provides a home for the short-tailed vole. The short-tailed vole has an important but unenviable role to play in the cycle of life here, in the Peak District, and elsewhere where it occurs. It is important as food for many creatures including foxes and kestrels and, as such, is an integral link in many food chains. The short-tailed vole is a small and dumpy mammal most easily distinguished from a mouse by the very short tail and the relatively small ears and thick neck. It lives in shallow runs just below the surface of fields and meadows.

50 Mole *Talpa europaea*
The most visible signs of the presence of moles in an area are the conspicuous molehills thrown up as the animal burrows through the surface soil. Sadly, this industrious activity is sometimes viewed with displeasure by landowners who go to great lengths to eradicate them. While a honeycombed field may not be good news for cattle, there is a more positive side to the mole's burrowing. Along with the earthworm, which comprises the major part of its diet, the mole is extremely good at aerating the soil which in turn leads to richer grassland.

51 Pygmy Shrew *Sorex minutus*
What the pygmy shrew lacks in size it makes up for in energy. This tireless creature searches throughout the day and night for insects, snails and other invertebrates with only short bouts of rest in between periods of frantic activity. Indeed, this frenetic behaviour is not a matter of choice but rather of necessity, for the pygmy shrew will die if it does not eat every couple of hours or so. Pygmy shrews, like others of their kind, have pointed noses and relatively short legs. They can be found almost anywhere where rank vegetation grows, such as hedgerows and scrub.

52 Harvest Mouse *Micromys minutus*
Our smallest mammal is also one of our most endearing. Although the harvest mouse has declined markedly in many parts of the country, probably due to changes in land usage, it is still fairly common in lowland parts of the Peak District. This does not mean it is easy to see, however, and the round nests, made from woven, shredded grasses, are found more often than the animal is observed. The harvest mouse has a coat which is golden-brown above and pale below. The tail, although not truly prehensile, can be used to grip grass stems and thus support the animal as it climbs.

53 Fox *Vulpes vulpes*
Foxes, although fairly common in the Peak District, are justifiably wary of man and hence are seen more by luck than anything else. You might be lucky enough to see one trotting through moorland cover on the other side of a valley, or catch one in car headlights while driving after dark. Foxes live underground, their home being referred to as an earth. Cubs are born in late winter and, in warm spring sunshine, may come out to play at the entrance during the afternoon. The entrance to an earth is usually well concealed among rank vegetation or scree and rock.

54 Badger *Meles meles*
Tracks, trails and signs of badgers are more usually found than the animals themselves are seen. They are mainly nocturnal and spend the day underground in their setts. Easily recognised by their black and white striped faces, badgers forage on the ground and a major part of their diet is earthworms; they will also take bulbs, beetles and other invertebrates if they can find them. These days, badgers are having a hard time thanks to man's activities. Many are killed on roads at night and even more face the threat of badger-baiting, a degrading and barbaric pursuit where a badger and a number of dogs are encouraged to fight to the death.

52

53

54

56

BUTTERFLIES

55 **Brimstone** *Gonepteryx rhamni*
You know that spring is on the way when you see your first
brimstone butterfly. These attractive insects hibernate through
the winter, often among dense clumps of ivy, and emerge
when the sun finally warms the air in March or April. Wooded
valleys, hedgerows and scrub are all suitable habitats to look
for brimstones; males are bright yellow while females are very
pale by comparison, often appearing almost white in bright
sunshine. The caterpillars feed on the leaves of alder
buckthorn and are difficult to find, having excellent
camouflage.

56 **Orange Tip** *Anthocharis cardamines*
Look for orange tips when bluebells begin to flower in
earnest, in early May. It is only the male that has the orange-
tipped wings, the forewings of the female being black instead.
When seen from the underside, the orange tip is equally
attractive. There is still an orange flush to the forewings of the
male but the underside is beautifully marbled with greenish
patterning. Orange tips can be found in open woodland and
along hedgerows. They are seldom seen far from areas where
their foodplant — garlic mustard — is common and females
can sometimes be seen laying the eggs on its leaves.

57 **Common Blue** *Polyommatus icarus*
Common blues are widespread in grassy places in the Peak District but are particularly numerous on lime-rich soils. Here, the foodplants of the caterpillar grow well; bird's-foot trefoil is the most usual species but other members of the pea family may also be eaten on occasions. The common blue is an active, sun-loving insect. Because broods are produced in succession, it can be seen on the wing from May until September in some years. It is only the male that has the blue upperwing, those of the female usually being brown. The underwings are grey-brown with dark spots.

58 **Small Skipper** *Thymelicus sylvestris*
This species can be recognised by its small size — it has a wingspan of 25mm — the orange-brown colour and rapid, buzzing wingbeats. It is a grassland species and especially common on lime-rich soils; the caterpillars eat grass leaves. Small skippers fly from May to August, specimens at the end of the season looking very worn indeed. On dull days, they sometimes sit around on grass stems and heads with their wings partly raised and swept back. On sunny days, they are very active and frequently visit flowers to feed on nectar. Males and females look rather similar.

59 Dark Green Fritillary *Mesocidalia aglaia*
In the Peak District, the dark green fritillary favours areas of
limestone grassland. Here, the foodplants of its caterpillars —
violets — thrive in the short turf. The dark green fritillary is
one of the region's most attractive butterflies. Its upperwings
are orange-brown and marked with a complex pattern of
black. The under-surface of the hindwing is green with
conspicuous white spots. It is an extremely active species
that seldom settles for very long and flies fast over the rolling
slopes; strong winds have seemingly little effect upon its
flight.

60 Small Heath *Coenonympha pamphilus*
This attractive little butterfly is a meadow species whose
caterpillars feed on grasses. Compared to many other
species of British butterfly, it has a weak flight and seldom
takes to the wing on dull days, preferring instead to rest
among low vegetation. The small heath is seen on the wing
from May to August. It has buffish-orange upperwings with a
dark border and a small dark eyespot near the angle of the
forewing. The underwings also show an eyespot on the
forewing; the hindwings are marbled with grey and dark
brown. The small heath is generally rather common.

60

61

Lead has been mined in the Peak District since at least Roman times, the lead ore occurring in veins in limestone rock.

From the peak of its activity in the 17th century, the industry declined until today, when most mines have long since been abandoned: all that remains of most former lead mines are the spoil tips.

Lead is notoriously toxic to most forms of life and few plants colonise the workings. Two species, however, thrive under these conditions: spring sandwort and mountain pansy are often common.

Upper: Alpine Pennycress Thlaspi Caerulescens
Lower: Spring Sandwort Minuartia verna gerardii

61 **White-letter Hairstreak** *Strymonidia w-album*
Throughout Britain and including the Peak District, the white-letter hairstreak is an extremely local butterfly. This is mainly because of its very precise habitat requirements: the caterpillars feed on the leaves of elms — wych elm in this part of the country — a tree that is local itself at the best of times and made more so by the ravages of Dutch elm disease. Where it does occur, this species can be quite numerous. The adults always remain on and around the host tree but sometimes visit bramble flowers to feed. White-letter hairstreaks fly in July and are named after the white letter 'w' on the underwing.

62

66

OTHER INSECTS

62 Dark Bush Cricket *Pholidoptera griseoaptera*
Although easily overlooked, the dark bush cricket is a common insect in many parts of the Peak District, preferring areas of scrubby grassland and roadside verges, especially where bramble flourishes.
The body of the dark bush cricket is about 20mm long and dark brown in colour. Like others of its kind, it is easily identified because of its exceptionally long antennae and very long hind legs. The female has a long, scythe-like ovipositor which, although it looks dangerous, is used solely for laying eggs in plant stems.

63 Meadow Grasshopper *Chorthippus parallelus*
The meadow grasshopper is the commonest and most widespread of several related species found in the Peak District. Young stages are seen in May and June with adults being a common sight in July and August. There is quite a difference in the size and appearance of the different sexes. The female is usually around 23mm long, with a rather swollen abdomen and wings reduced to a small size and useless for flight. The male is considerably smaller, usually 15mm in length, and has functional wings. The meadow grasshopper is very varied in colour.

64 Common Field Grasshopper
Chorthippus brunneus

As with the meadow grasshopper, female common field grasshoppers are considerably bigger than males, usually being 27mm or so in length as opposed to 20mm in the male. Both sexes are usually brownish in colour with dark markings on the wings and body. This species is extremely active and flies vigorously for short distances on sunny days. Males sing loudly during the summer months by rubbing their legs against their wings. The common field grasshopper is mainly a grassland species and is locally common in suitable habitats.

65 Common Green Grasshopper *Omocestus viridulus*

At first glance, this species may seem rather similar to the common field grasshopper. It does, however, invariably show a green stripe running along the dorsal surface of the head, thorax and wings. If you study the markings which border the dorsal surface of the thorax — the middle section of the body — you will see a gently incurved black line. In the common field grasshopper, this forms a sharp angle. Like other species of grasshoppers, it feeds mainly on grass and other meadow plants. It can be very difficult to spot on dull days since it remains inactive.

66 Seven-spot Ladybird
Coccinella 7-punctata

This familiar ladybird is in fact only one of several species that occur in the Peak District. It is, however, the most common and widespread and can be found from May to September in most years. The adults are easily recognised by the red and shiny wing cases which form the most obvious part of the insect's body; seven black spots give it its vernacular name. Both as adults and during their larval stages, ladybirds are voracious predators, their favourite prey being aphids. The larvae, which are orange and black and with awesome piercing jaws, are seemingly insatiable. Gardeners have good reason to be grateful to this insect.

67 Common Woodlouse *Oniscus asellus*
Turn over almost any stone on the ground in the Peak District
and a range of tiny creatures will go scurrying away. Some of
these will be woodlice, especially in areas of limestone, and
the most frequently encountered of these, as its name
suggests, is the common woodlouse. Woodlice are crustacea
— related to crabs and prawns — that are adapted to life on
land. The body is protected from above by armoured plates
on each of the segments. They are vulnerable to desiccation
and seldom venture out of cover except after dark or on wet
days.

68 Large Black Slug *Arion ater*
On damp or rainy days — all too frequent in the Peak District
— large black slugs are a frequent sight on paths, tracks,
moors and grassland. These large shell-less molluscs, which
can reach a length of 8cm or more, leave a trail of shiny
mucus wherever they go. The mucus enables the underside of
their body to get a grip on the substrate and eases their
passage. Clusters of translucent eggs are laid in the autumn
and can sometimes be found by turning over stones.
Occasionally the parental slug can also be found in
attendance.

69 Centipede *Lithobius variegatus*
Woodland leaf litter and hedgerows are home to this
centipede, one of several species that occurs in the Peak
District. Like others of its kind, it has a pair of legs on each
of the segments, these being rather flattened and shiny
golden-brown in colour. The head of the centipede carries a
fearsome set of jaws which soon dispel any thought of these
invertebrates being benign members of the woodland floor
community. They are active predators and will take insect
larvae and almost anything else of a similar size to
themselves.

TREES AND SHRUBS

70 Silver Birch *Betula pendula*
The silver birch is a common tree in the Peak District. With its
rapid growth, it is one which is quick to colonise and can be
found encroaching on moorland areas and in damp valleys.
A fully mature tree can grow to a height of 25m or more,
although most specimens are much smaller. Trees of
moderate size have silvery-white bark with deep fissures but
this becomes gnarled with age. In the spring, the young
leaves are an attractive, fresh green while in the autumn whole
trees can turn golden yellow for a few days before the leaves
start to drop.

71 Sessile Oak *Quercus petraea*
In mature, natural woodlands, the sessile oak is often the
commonest tree in Peak District valleys where the underlying
soils are acid. A full grown tree may exceed 30m in height but
most are considerably smaller than this in the region. The
leaves are typically oak-like in outline. Unlike Britain's other
native oak, the English oak, they are carried on short stalks.
The acorns, on the other hand, are stalkless — hence 'sessile'
oak — in contrast to those of its close relative. Oaks of both
species are important for wildlife and support more insect
species than any other species of native tree.

72 Rowan *Sorbus aucuparia*
Also known as mountain ash, this species is common in the
Peak District. The leaves are pinnately divided and, as you
might expect from the name, bear a superficial resemblance
to those of the ash. Those of the mountain ash do, however,
have rounded, almost oval leaflets and not pointed ones.
In the spring, rowan produces dense clusters of white flowers.
These eventually become bright red berries which, in the
autumn, provide a harvest for many of the birds of the region.
As well as growing wild, rowan is also commonly planted in
gardens and along roadsides.

73 Field Maple *Acer campestre*
Field maple grows commonly in hedgerows, sometimes as a
small tree, reaching a height of 15m or so, but more usually
as a shrub. For much of the year, it is overlooked by passers-
by but it comes into its own in the autumn. For a few weeks,
generally during September or early October, the leaves turn
a beautiful golden-yellow, a colour which is quite distinct from
other hedgerow shrubs and trees. This is also the time of year
to look for the seeds which are carried in fused pairs, each
partner having a broad wing; these assist their dispersal by
the wind.

74 **Bird Cherry** *Prunus padus*
In the Peak District, bird cherry can be found growing as an understorey tree in ash woodlands and in scrub on lime-rich soils. It seldom reaches a height of more than 10m and is often overlooked. Except, that is, in May when the tree bursts into flower: the branches are covered in long sprays of white flowers, the individual flowers having five rounded petals. In the autumn, blackish, hard-stoned berries are produced; these are too bitter for our tastes but are relished by birds, hence the tree's name. The leaves are oval in outline and pointed.

75 **Ash** *Fraxinus excelsior*
On limestone soils in the Peak District, ash is usually the dominant tree in wooded areas, growing to a height of 30m or so. Ash leaves are pinnately divided and comprise usually seven to 11 leaflets, each one of which is roughly oval and pointed; there is a single, terminal leaflet but the remaining ones are carried in opposite pairs. The tree produces bunches of winged seeds in autumn; when they fall, they can be carried by the wind for a considerable distance. Ash bark is grey and highly fissured and ridged in mature specimens. The twigs are flattened at the nodes.

75

*The Peak National Park lies
at the southern end of the Pennines,
a chain of uplands that stretches
from here northwards
to the border counties.*

A long distance trail — the Pennine Way
— follows this upland course and,
depending on the starting point of the
visitor, either begins or ends in Edale.
During its short length within the park, the
Pennine Way crosses some of the region's
most expansive stretches of moorland.

Upper: Hairstail Cottongrass Eriophorum Vaginatum

76 Hazel *Corylus avellana*
Hazel is a common shrub of hedgerows, scrub and open woodland, growing especially well where the underlying soil is lime-rich. The catkins, which often appear as early as January, are long and yellow; the leaves are produced subsequently and are broadly oval with a toothed margin. The nuts, which ripen in the autumn, are the familiar hazelnuts. When they fall to the ground, and indeed before this, they provide a rich harvest for small mammals in particular. Hazel rarely grows to a height of more than 8m and is usually classed as a shrub rather than a tree.

77 Hawthorn *Crataegus monogyna*
Visit the Peak District in spring and you see fine displays of hawthorn, especially in areas where the soils are lime-rich. 'May blossom' is a local name for this shrub which is indeed covered with white flowers during this month; individual flowers are five-petalled. The bright-red berries start to ripen in the summer and remain visible until either consumed by birds or damaged by frost. Hawthorn is a typical hedgerow shrub but is also an important component of scrubland in the country. The spiny branches provide a sanctuary for nesting songbirds.

78 Dogwood *Cornus sanguinea*
Dogwood is a common shrub found in hedgerows and scrub in the Peak District, especially where the underlying soil is lime-rich. It can be recognised even during the winter months by its distinctive red twigs. The leaves of dogwood are oval and pointed at the tip; the upper surface is shiny and dark green, with only a few veins. Between May and July, flat-topped clusters of off-white flowers are produced, the individual flowers having four petals. In the autumn, blackish berries are produced and are soon eaten by hungry birds.

WILDFLOWERS

79 Greater Stitchwort *Stellaria holostea*
From April to June, hedgerows and woodlands burst into life as spring flowers come into bloom. A casual glance almost anywhere except on the most acid soils is likely to reveal sprays of greater stitchwort, the flowers resembling miniature stars among the green foliage. Greater stitchwort grows in a rather sprawling fashion among other vegetation. The leaves are grass-like and have rough edges. The flowers are up to 30mm across and comprise five white petals that are divided almost to the base, thereby giving the impression of ten petals.

80 Red Campion *Silene dioica*
The pinkish-red flowers of red campion are a common sight along hedgerows, lanes, roadside borders and woodland tracks in the Peak District. Although most flowers appear between June and August, the plant has an extremely extended flowering period and the occasional flower can be found in almost any month. The flowers comprise five petals which are deeply notched. The stems are rather twiggy and usually downy; in some plants they can feel slightly sticky. In suitable areas, red campion can form extensive patches.

85

82

81 Meadow Buttercup *Ranunculus acris*
Undisturbed meadows in the Peak District where herbicides have not been applied can sometimes turn yellow with the flowers of meadow buttercup. One of several closely related species found here, this is the most widespread in the region. Meadow buttercup is a rather straggly plant. Its flowers, roughly 20mm across, are borne on long stalks and comprise five bright-yellow petals. The leaves, and especially those on the stem, are highly divided; those lower down are carried on stalks. Meadow buttercup flowers from April to August, with a peak in flowering in May and June.

82 Globeflower *Trollius europaeus*
Without doubt, the globeflower is the most impressive member of the buttercup family to be found in the Peak District. It is also a well-named plant because the flowers are indeed globe shaped. The appearance of the flower is, however, slightly misleading since it comprises bright yellow sepals, the petals being reduced and concealed inside the orb. Globeflower grows in damp meadows and in wet flushes beside rivers; flowers appear from May to July. The plant has a mainly northern distribution and finds one of its southernmost outposts in the Peak District.

83 Wood Anemone *Anemone nemorosa*
One of the most attractive sights in the spring woodland is that of wood anemones growing in profusion. In some areas in the Peak District, mainly in ash woods on lime-rich soils, an almost continuous carpet is formed where soil and light conditions suit it well. The leaves are deep green and palmately divided. The flowers are characteristic of anemones as a group in appearance. What appear to be petals are in fact sepals; they are white, usually six to ten in number and the flowers are roughly 30-40mm across. Wood anemone flowers during April and May.

84 Biting Stonecrop *Sedum acre*
Stonecrops are often found growing in seemingly uninviting places for plants and this species is no exception. Biting stonecrop is a low-growing, mat-forming plant that is evergreen and is found on walls and rocky outcrops; it is rather local in the Peak District but easily seen where it does occur. The fleshy-looking leaves are packed tightly up the stems. From May to July, attractive, star-shaped flowers are produced; they are bright yellow and comprise five petals. The plant gets its name from the rather peppery taste of its leaves.

85 Opposite-leaved Golden-saxifrage *Chrysosplenium oppositifolium*
Damp, shady habitats are needed for opposite-leaved golden-saxifrage to flourish. In the Peak District, suitable conditions are provided along the banks of streams, in wet woodland flushes and in water run-offs beside rocky outcrops. In isolation, the plant is comparatively insignificant. However, it often grows in sizeable patches when the yellow, petal-less flowers put on a fine show. As the name suggests, the leaves are carried in opposite pairs; they are rounded, toothed and slightly hairy. Flowers appear from April to June.

86 Tormentil *Potentilla erecta*

Grassy places, roadside verges and moors in the Peak District are often studded with the small but delightful flowers of tormentil. These are bright yellow, 7-10mm across and comprise four petals which are easily dislodged. Tormentil flowers from May until August but individual flowers do not persist for very long. The plant itself is rather straggly and trailing; it carries trifoliate, unstalked leaves which have toothed margins and are slightly downy around the margins. Tormentil is common in most parts of the Peak District.

87 Cloudberry *Rubus chamaemorus*

Cloudberry is a plant that is characteristic of moorland habitats. Although not especially common in the Peak District, it is nevertheless regularly encountered by walkers. The flowers superficially resemble those of bramble, to which this species is related. They are white, up to 25mm across and are borne singly on upright stalks. In the summer months, the orange fruit develops and, in shape, recalls a raspberry. Each individual plant has no more than three leaves, although growing side by side, fairly large patches can be formed.

88 Dropwort *Filipendula vulgaris*

Grassy meadows where the underlying soil is lime-rich offer the best opportunities for seeing dropwort; this member of the rose family is locally common in such areas within the Peak District. When not in flower, the plant is easily overlooked. The leaves are pinnately divided and usually comprise 10-20 leaflets. The flowers appear from May to August and are carried in dense clusters which are rather flat-topped and triangular in outline. Individual flowers are creamy white above and reddish below; they have a heady fragrance.

89 Bramble *Rubus fruticosus*

The ubiquitous bramble needs little introduction and is widespread within the Peak District. It can be found in all sorts of habitats, except perhaps the bleakest moorland summits, and thrives best in hedgerows, areas of scrub and woodland clearings and rides. Among the most noticeable features of this rambling, woody shrub are its prickles. The leaves are also sometimes prickly and comprise three to five toothed leaflets. The flowers, which appear from May to August, are white or pink with five petals. From August onwards, clusters of blackberries are produced.

90 Wild Strawberry *Fragaria vesca*

Ripe wild strawberries have a mouth-watering taste. The only trouble is their small size — finding enough of them to make it worthwhile can be a problem. The plant is low-growing and produces trifoliate leaves, the leaflets being toothed. Small white flowers, comprising five petals, are produced from April to July and the tiny fruits, often less than 10mm long, develop thereafter; at first they are green but they turn red as they ripen. Wild strawberry is a plant which thrives best on lime-rich soils and can be found in grassland and hedgerows.

91 Herb Bennet *Geum urbanum*

Also known as wood avens, this is a plant of shady spots along hedgerows and woodland tracks, and also of grassy scrub. The leaves are pinnately lobed at the base but comprise three leaflets up the stem. The flowers are small, roughly 10-15mm across, and appear from May to August; they comprise five yellow petals and five sepals. The fruits which develop subsequently have hook-tipped projections which catch in the fur of passing animals; in this way, the dispersal of the seeds is greatly assisted. Wood avens is common and widespread in suitable habitats in the Peak District.

92 Common Lady's-mantle *Alchemilla glabra*

This is a plant that will be familiar to many gardeners since allied species are often grown in cultivation. Common lady's-mantle is extremely variable and indeed the species is further divided by many taxonomists. Typically, it has leaves which bear angular lobes, the surfaces of which are hairless. The individual flowers, such as they are, are small and greenish-yellow. They are produced in rather globular clusters and appear from June to September. Common lady's-mantle grows in grassland and grassy scrub. In the Peak District, it is most often seen on lime-rich soils.

93 Common Gorse *Ulex europaeus*

Within the Peak District, gorse is a common plant of moorland habitats. In actual fact, two closely related species are found in the region. Common gorse flowers mainly in May and June while its ally, western gorse, flowers from July to September. Because of extended flowering periods and overlap between the species, if you search hard enough you can find a few gorse flowers at almost any time of year. Common gorse is extremely spiny and has small, trifoliate leaves. The rich yellow flowers are produced in terminal clusters and smell of coconut.

94 Broom *Cytisus scoparius*

Broom is characterised at all times of the year by its long, twiggy stems that are five-angled. Unlike its cousin, gorse, the plant is not spiny. Small, trifoliate leaves are produced in the spring, followed by the large and showy yellow flowers, 20mm long, whose shape is typical of members of the pea family. Later in the season, blackish pods are produced which eventually split and liberate the seeds. Broom is a plant that grows best on acid soils; in the Peak District, it can be found in areas of scrub and along hedgerows, too.

95 Bird's-foot Trefoil *Lotus corniculatus*

Within the Peak District, bird's-foot trefoil can be found growing in grassy places of all sorts, although the plant perhaps does best where the underlying soil is lime-rich. It is rather variable in appearance but always has leaves that appear trifoliate; in fact they are pinnately divided but the lower two leaflets resemble bracts. The flowers, which appear from June to September, are yellow, sometimes tinged orange, and carried in heads of two to five. These subsequently ripen into long seed pods whose arrangement fancifully resembles the foot of a bird.

96 Wood Sorrel *Oxalis acetosella*
Wood sorrel is an enchanting plant that is locally common in the Peak District, favouring woodlands, particularly where ash predominates. The trifoliate leaves are shamrock-like and are carried on long stalks. In some areas, where conditions of light and drainage suit the plant, wood sorrel can form extensive carpets. The leaves, however, often grow in greater profusion than the flowers which appear from April to June. These are whitish with a beautiful network of purple veins on the petals; they are carried on long stalks and often droop slightly.

97 Meadow Crane's-bill *Geranium pratense*
Seen growing in profusion, this is one of the most attractive plants to be found in and around the Peak District. Meadow crane's-bill, as its name suggests, is a grassland plant but is also commonly seen along roadside verges; it thrives best on lime-rich soils. The leaves are broad and extremely divided, usually with six or seven lobes. The flowers are 25-30mm across and are bluish in colour, sometimes the colour having a hint of purple; they are paired and carried on long stalks. Meadow crane's-bill flowers between June and September.

98 Bloody Crane's-bill *Geranium sanguineum*
In the Peak District, bloody crane's-bill is a plant almost exclusively found on lime-rich soils, growing in limestone grassland. The leaves are rounded but are deeply divided into five to seven lobes; they are up to 50mm across. The flowers, which comprise five petals and are 25-30mm across, are a deep reddish-purple colour, deserving of the name 'bloody'; the petals are easily dislodged. The flowers are carried on long stalks and can be seen from June to August. Bloody crane's-bill is locally common in the region and, in suitable grassy habitats, can spread widely.

STONE IN THE PEAK DISTRICT

Although varied in character throughout the region, stone hewn from the ground in the Peak District has long been of importance to its inhabitants.

The classic example of this is perhaps the sandstone which was carved into the famous millstones, now a symbol of the National Park, and giving their name to the rock itself. Abandoned examples in various stages of preparation can be seen in suitable areas throughout the park. Equally conspicuous are limestone walls, constructed in regions where the underlying rocks are of this type.

Upper: Limestone walls
Lower: Curbar Edge

99 **Herb Robert** *Geranium robertianum*

Herb Robert has a long flowering period and can be found in flower in the Peak District at any time from April to late September. It is a plant of damp, shady places and grows in hedgerows, banks and woodlands. The plant is rather straggling with leaves that divide into five lobes and look rather fern like; both leaves and stems are often tinged with red. The flowers are pale pink and roughly 15mm across. They comprise five petals but some or all of these are often missing or dislodged, making this number somewhat academic.

102 Perforate St John's-wort *Hypericum perforatum*
Perforate St John's-wort is the most showy and widespread of several allied species found in the Peak District region; it is also reminiscent of cultivated relatives. Growing among scrub and grassland on lime-rich soils, it reaches a height of 60cm or more. The stem bears two lines on opposite sides along its length and the oval leaves are studded with translucent dots. The flowers, which appear from June to September, are bright yellow and comprise five petals; there are usually black dots along the margins of the petals and on the sepals.

103 Mountain Pansy *Viola lutea*
Mountain pansy is an attractive upland flower, worthy of any cultivated rockery. In the Peak District it grows wild and is locally common in moorland grassland, and it is tolerant of soils which range from neutral to lime-rich. The leaves are alternate and there are also leaf-like stipules which are divided into three to five segments. The attractive flowers are up to 30mm across and are carried on long stalks; they are a distinctive mixture of yellow, purple and off-white. Mountain pansy flowers from May to July and is locally common.

104 Common Dog-violet *Viola riviniana*
The attractive purple flowers of common dog-violet sometimes appear as early as March and flowering continues in succession until June. It grows in grassy places and can be found in hedgerows and grassland, on roadside verges and along grassy woodland rides. The leaves are heart-shaped and carried on long stalks. They are arranged in a rosette around which the flowering stems are produced; these bear the deep purple flowers which are 25mm across with a pale, backward-pointing spur. Common dog-violet is widespread and frequent in the Peak District.

105 Common Rock-rose *Helianthemum nummularium*
Common rock-rose is a plant of limestone grassland in the Peak District and, as such, is locally common. In some areas, where it grows unchecked by grazing or cutting, it almost forms low shrubs. The leaves are oval-lanceolate in outline, with a woolly under-surface and inrolled margins. The flowers, which appear from June to September, are bright yellow and up to 25mm across. They comprise five petals which are soft and rather like crumpled tissue paper; these are very easily dislodged, even falling after heavy rain or strong winds.

100 Kidney Vetch *Anthyllis vulneraria*
When in flower, generally between May and August, kidney vetch can put on a showy display since it sometimes grows in surprising profusion. Its pinnately divided leaves are covered in silky hairs and are usually rather folded back along the keel. The yellow flowers are carried in dense, rounded heads which are produced in tightly-packed pairs. As they die back, the flowers assume a rusty-brown colour. Kidney vetch is a plant of grassy places and is most frequently seen on lime-rich soils in the Peak District; it is locally common.

101 Dog's mercury *Mercurialis perennis*
Although dog's mercury is neither showy nor especially attractive, it is, nevertheless, an important woodland plant. In ash woods in the Peak District it can form extensive stands on the floor, sometimes locally to the exclusion of almost all other plants in areas where conditions suit it. Dog's mercury produces an upright stem on which oval, pointed leaves are carried. Plants are either male or female. Spikes of male flowers are carried on long stalks, while those of females are on short stalks; flowering occurs from February to April.

106 Hogweed *Heracleum sphondylium*
Several superficially similar members of the carrot family grow in the Peak District but, of these, hogweed is the most robust and widespread. The plant is hairy and produces tall, hollow stems which are distinctly ridged. The leaves are divided into several leaflets which are oval in outline and toothed. From May to August, large umbels of flowers are produced at the top of the stems. These are flat-topped, usually more than 15cm across and comprise large numbers of tiny white flowers. Hogweed grows in grassy and wayside places such as roadside verges, hedgerows and grassland.

107 Ling *Calluna vulgaris*
If you want to see the moors of the Peak District at their very best, then visit the area in July and August. At this time of year the ling — or simply 'heather' as it is sometimes referred to — will be in bloom, turning whole hillsides pinkish-purple with its flowers. The plant forms low, evergreen shrubs which become the dominant vegetation in some areas. The leaves are small and needle-like and are carried in four rows up the stem. The bell-like flowers are roughly 4mm long and are carried in spikes which are rather one-sided.

108 Cross-leaved Heath *Erica tetralix*
Cross-leaved heath can sometimes be found growing side by side with ling but generally prefers much damper areas of moorland than its relative. As its name suggests, the leaves are arranged in groups of fours up the stem; individually, they are narrow and needle-like. The attractive flowers are pale pink and arranged in clusters at the ends of stems. Individual flowers are egg-shaped, the opening being extremely constricted. Cross-leaved heath is locally common in suitable habitats in the Peak District and flowers between June and August.

109 Bell Heather *Erica cinerea*

Like its relative ling, bell heather can sometimes become rather dominant in the moorland habitats where it flourishes. It forms a low-growing shrub which comprises fairly compact groups of leafy spikes. The individual leaves are narrow and needle-like; they are arranged in groups of three up the stem. From June to September, taller spikes of purple flowers are produced. Individual flowers are 5mm long and are egg-shaped with a narrowly constricted opening. Bell heather prefers dry moorland areas and is locally common in the Peak District.

110 Cowberry *Vaccinium vitis-idaea*

For much of the year, cowberry can be easily overlooked, growing as it does in areas where the more common bilberry often thrives. In the early summer, however, during June and July, it produces distinctive flowers which make it easier to recognise. These are pale pink and bell-shaped, with a protruding style, and are carried in clusters. Later in the season, shiny red berries form in their place. Cowberry leaves are oval and leathery; they are retained throughout the year. Cowberry is locally fairly common on damp moors in the Peak District.

111 Bilberry *Vaccinium myrtillus*

Also sometimes known as whortleberry, this is a plant of damp moorland, bogs and lightly wooded areas on acid soils. Bilberry grows to form low shrubs with a rather twiggy appearance to the three-angled stems. The leaves are fresh green and toothed. The flowers are superficially berry-like: they are reddish, almost spherical and with a fairly wide opening. They appear from April to June and are followed subsequently by the formation of the real berries which are blue-black, covered in a bloom and delicious to eat.

112 Primrose *Primula vulgaris*

Hedgerows, roadside verges and woodland rides in the Peak District are often adorned with colourful clumps of primroses in the spring. These sometimes appear as early as March but are generally at their best in April and May, thriving particularly well where the underlying soil is lime-rich. Primroses have a rosette of long, spoon-shaped leaves with a wrinkly surface. From the centre of the rosette, long stalks carry the familiar flowers which are usually 25mm across; these comprise five yellow petals and the flowers are popular with pollinating insects.

110

111

113 Cowslip *Primula veris*

Cowslips are as common on areas of limestone grassland in the Peak District as they are anywhere in the country. The leaves are long and spoon-shaped with a wrinkled surface, and are produced as a basal rosette. From the centre of the rosette, a number of tall stalks are produced bearing a terminal cluster of yellow flowers. Individual flowers are rather drooping and have relatively small but spreading petals. The flowers appear during April and May; after they die, the dried, withered remains persist for some time. Cowslips also grow on roadside verges and along woodland rides.

114 Yellow Pimpernel *Lysimachia nemorum*

Damp, grassy areas with considerable shade and bare soil are ideal for yellow pimpernel. The plant is evergreen, low-growing and is sometimes prostrate on the ground. The leaves are bright green and pointed, and carried in opposite pairs along the stems. From May to August, attractive yellow flowers, up to 15mm across, are produced; they are carried on longish stalks from the leaf axils and comprise five petals. Yellow pimpernel is fairly common in the Peak District and can be found growing in meadows and hedgerows, and sometimes along roadside verges.

115 Bogbean *Menyanthes trifoliata*

Bogbean is a distinctive wetland plant that thrives both in shallow water and boggy flushes. Much of the plant will actually grow in water but the leaves grow above the surface. They are trifoliate and, as the plant's common name suggests, resemble those of the broad bean not only in shape, but also in colour and texture. In the spring the plant

produces erect flower stems. From April to June, these carry tall but dense spikes of flowers which are white, star-shaped and fringed with conspicuous hairs. Bogbean is locally common in the Peak District.

116 Heath Bedstraw *Galium saxatile*
As the name suggests, bedstraws were indeed once used as bedding material for mattresses. Of those that occur in the Peak District region, heath bedstraw is the most widespread of the white-flowering species. It is common in moorland settings, preferring acid soils and avoiding lime-rich ones. Heath bedstraw is low-growing and spreading, sometimes climbing through and up neighbouring vegetation. The leaves are narrow and lanceolate, bearing forward-pointing bristles on the margins. The white flowers are arranged in dense clusters and the whole plant turns black when dry.

117 Lady's Bedstraw *Galium verum*
Lady's bedstraw is a plant of grassland and hedgerows and, in the Peak District, is most commonly associated with areas of limestone grassland. It is comparatively easy to recognise, being the only true bedstraw in the region with yellow flowers. The plant sprawls amongst the general ground vegetation but also produces upright stems on which the terminal flower clusters or spikes are borne; the individual flowers are deep yellow and tightly packed. The dark green leaves are narrow and tipped with a spine; they are arranged in whorls along the stem.

SLUGS AND SNAILS

The shell of a snail is constructed in the main from calcium carbonate, the chemical basis for limestone. It is not surprising, therefore, that these creatures are far more numerous where the underlying rocks are calcium-rich rather than on acid soils.

They are best searched for in limestone grassland on wet days and in crevices in stone walls. Slugs, shell-less relatives of snails, are also numerous. Look out for the tree slug in wooded areas. In damp weather it climbs up the trunks.

Upper: White-lipped Snail Cepaea hortensis
Lower: Tree Slug Limax marginatus

118 Crosswort *Cruciata laevipes*

Although not strictly speaking a true bedstraw, crosswort does belong to the same family and bears a passing resemblance to lady's bedstraw. Like that species, it too is a plant of grassy places such as meadows and roadside verges, and is most often found on limestone grassland in the Peak District. The plant is partly creeping but produces upright stems, up to 50cm high. These bear whorls of four oval leaves in the shape of a cross; both leaves and stems are hairy. The attractive yellow flowers are each four-lobed and are grouped in clusters in the axils of the leaves.

119 Jacob's-ladder *Polemonium caeruleum*

To find Jacob's-ladder on a visit to the Peak District would be the highlight of the trip for most botanical visitors. This is very much a speciality plant of the region and has the centre of its British distribution on limestone soils in the Peak District. Jacob's-ladder grows to a height of 80cm or more. The tall stems bear pinnately divided leaves, each comprising six to 12 leaflets. The attractive flowers are produced in clusters at the end of the stem. They are blue, 25-30mm across and comprise five petals with protruding style and stamens.

120 Wood Sage *Teucrium scoradonia*

An aptly-named plant since it is often found growing in woods and its leaves are indeed sage-like in appearance. Wood sage is a member of the mint family and is an upright, downy plant usually growing to a height of 50cm. The leaves are roughly oval in outline but heart-shaped at the base; they have an intricately patterned texture. Spikes of flowers appear from July to September. The spikes comprise pairs of flowers each arising from bract axils; the flowers themselves are creamy yellow. Wood sage is fairly common in the Peak District, growing in woodland clearings and rides.

121 Bugle *Ajuga reptans*

The robust spikes of bugle are a familiar sight in the Peak District in the spring. Often forming quite large patches, the plant produces upright flowering stems. These carry oval-shaped leaves which are stalked at the base but stalkless further up the stem and arranged in opposite pairs; both stem and leaves are often strongly tinged with purple. The shape of the flowers is typical of members of the mint family. They are violet-purple and arranged in whorls above the leaves. Bugle flowers from April to June and is common on roadside verges, grassy places and woodland rides.

122 Ground Ivy *Glechoma hederacea*

Ground ivy is a rather variable plant. Sometimes it grows in a compact form and carpets large areas of ground; in other areas the plants are taller, less leafy and with fewer flowers. The plant is hairy and creeping but produces upright stems to a height of 20cm, though often much less. The leaves are kidney-shaped with toothed margins and are carried on stalks. The flowers are 20mm long, bluish-purple and are produced in whorls of two to four. Ground ivy flowers from March to June and grows in a wide variety of habitats including grassland, roadside verges and woodland.

123 Yellow Archangel *Lamiastrum galeobdolon*

Yellow archangel is an attractive spring flower that is locally common in the Peak District. The plant produces upright flowering stems which, before the flowers appear, have a texture and appearance recalling that of nettle. The leaves are broadly oval and jaggedly toothed. The flowers are yellow with darker markings; they are produced in whorls and are popular with pollinating insects. Yellow archangel grows best on base-rich soils and so, in the Peak District is often, but not always, found on limestone soils. It grows in hedgerows and along woodland rides.

124 Selfheal *Prunella vulgaris*

Selfheal is a plant of grassy places and, in the Peak District, occurs in meadows, open woodlands and along roadside verges. It is a more or less creeping plant which produces upright flowering stems. These carry oval leaves which are downy to touch and arranged in pairs. The flowers are bluish purple and up to 15mm long and appear from June to September. They are borne in distinctive terminal heads which are compact, with purple hairy bracts. At any given time, each head carries relatively few flowers. Selfheal grows best on lime-rich soils and avoids acid ones.

122

123

124

120

125 Marjoram *Origanum vulgare*

Marjoram is a classic herb of base-rich soils and, in the Peak District, thrives on grassland and open scrub on limestone. The plant forms fairly loose clumps up to 60cm high. The stems carry relatively small, oval leaves which are extremely aromatic when bruised or rubbed, producing the familiar smell of culinary marjoram. The attractive pink flowers are carried in dense terminal clusters, and sometimes in whorls lower down the stem; the calyx is darker red in colour. Flowering occurs from July to September and marjoram is popular with pollinating insects.

126 Foxglove *Digitalis purpurea*

Surely among Britain's most attractive and most easily recognised plants, the foxglove is a familiar sight in many parts of the Peak District. The plant is usually a biennial, rosettes of large, oval leaves appearing in the first year and in the second producing flowering spikes. The upper surface of the leaves is downy and the margins are slightly toothed. From May to July, a succession of purple flowers is produced at the end of the stem. These are the familiar, slightly flattened tubes which are pendent and popular with bumblebees. Foxglove grows best on acid soils and is found in woodland clearings and hedgerows.

127 Lousewort *Pedicularis sylvatica*

The rather unappealing common name of this plant belies the attractive appearance of its flowers when viewed close-up. Lousewort is a plant of damp, boggy sites on moors and sometimes in grassy places, but invariably on poor, acid soils. It grows to a height of 15cm or so, but often much less, and is usually extremely branched. The leaves are deeply divided, the lobes having toothed margins. The flowers are pinkish-purple with a flattened, lobed lower lip and a curved and hooded upper lip. Lousewort flowers between May and July.

128 Yellow-rattle *Rhinanthus minor*

The intriguingly named yellow-rattle is so-called because the dry inflated base of the flower actually rattles when ripened and with seeds inside. The plant is semi-parasitic, gaining part of its nutrition from grassland plants. The leaves are linear and toothed and the leaf-like bracts are more triangular in outline. The flowers, which appear from May to August, are yellow with a hooded upper lip. Yellow-rattle grows in grassy places and, in the Peak District, is a plant of limestone grassland. It is locally common in the region.

125

126

127

129 Eyebright *Euphrasia nemorosa*

Although all aspects of this plant are seemingly in miniature, it is extremely attractive when studied closely. Eyebright is a rather variable plant and the species is further divided into separate species by some botanists. It is a semi-parasite, gaining at least part of its nutrition from other plants. Eyebright is usually much-branched, with close-packed leaves that are lobed and toothed. The flowers are often white but show yellow and purple markings; the spreading lower lip is divided into three lobes. The plant grows in grassy places and, in the Peak District, thrives best on limestone soils.

130 Common Butterwort *Pinguicula vulgaris*

Look for common butterwort in boggy places in the Peak District's moorland regions. It is not a plant that can tolerate competition from rank vegetation and often grows on bare areas of peat or moss, especially where standing or trickling water is present. Common butterwort is usually first located by its fresh green leaves that are arranged as a basal rosette. They have sticky surfaces which trap and digest insects: this is one of Britain's few carnivorous plants. The plant produces a flower stalk and solitary, purple flowers can be found between May and July.

131 Honeysuckle *Lonicera periclymenum*

Take an evening stroll along a country lane from June to August and the heady fragrance of honeysuckle flowers pervades the air wherever this climbing plant grows. It actually grows in a variety of settings, sometimes sprawling through hedgerows and elsewhere climbing trees. The oval leaves are produced in opposite pairs and first appear in bud as early as January. The flowers are whitish and arranged in whorls. These later develop into juicy red berries in the late summer which provide a feast for birds. Honeysuckle is common in the Peak District in woodland and hedgerows.

128

129

130

131

132 Harebell *Campanula rotundifolia*

133 Devil's-bit Scabious *Succisa pratensis*

134 Field Scabious *Knautia arvensis*

132 Harebell *Campanula rotundifolia*

At the slightest breeze, the delicate flowers of harebell nod and sway in a most becoming fashion. This is a plant of grassy places and, in the Peak District, thrives best where the underlying soil is lime-rich. The basal leaves of the plant are rounded and carried on stalks. The stem leaves, however, are grass-like and easily overlooked if the plant is not in bloom. The flowers are blue and bell-shaped with spreading, triangular lobes at the mouth. They are carried on slender stalks and in loose heads. Harebell flowers from July to September.

133 Devil's-bit Scabious *Succisa pratensis*

Although never particularly abundant, devil's-bit scabious is still a fairly common plant in Peak District grasslands. Each plant bears a number of basal leaves which rather are spoon-shaped in appearance; those up the stems are more oval in outline. Devil's-bit scabious produces flower heads on tall stalks, sometimes more than 50cm high. The heads are roughly 20mm across and are domed and almost hemispherical. They comprise a number of bluish-purple florets each with protruding anthers. Devil's-bit scabious flowers from June to September.

134 Field Scabious *Knautia arvensis*

Field scabious is an attractive grassland plant which, in the Peak District, is most commonly found in limestone areas. There are numerous basal leaves which are up to 15cm long, spoon-shaped and with slightly toothed margins. These, and the pinnately divided stem leaves, are roughly hairy. Long stalks, up to 70cm high, carry the rather flattened heads of flowers. These are 35mm across and pale bluish-lilac in colour; characteristically the outer flowers in the head are larger and spreading. Field scabious flowers from July to September.

135 Sheep's-bit *Jasione montana*

At first glance, the flowers of sheep's-bit are rather similar to those of devil's-bit scabious. Both are carried in rounded, rather globular heads but only devil's-bit has protruding stamens with the terminal anthers at right angles to the filaments, looking like hammer heads. Sheep's-bit is also a grassland species but, unlike the unrelated devil's-bit, seldom if ever occurs on lime-rich soils. Flowers can be found from May to August and the plant has a basal rosette of hairy, lanceolate leaves with wavy margins, and short, linear stem leaves.

136 Goldenrod *Solidago virgaurea*

Goldenrod is a rather unusual plant in that it grows in a wide variety of habitats and is tolerant of a range of soil types. Most of its leaves grow from the base and are spoon-shaped in outline. Smaller and smaller leaves appear up the stem, these being more lanceolate in outline. The branched clusters of flowers are carried on solitary stalks which are slender but surprisingly robust. The individual flower heads are yellow, daisy-like and up to 10mm across. Goldenrod flowers from June to September and is locally common in the Peak District. It grows in grassland but also in shady places, sometimes beside water.

CEMENT AND SHALE

Exploitation of the earth's resources still continues within the boundaries of the Peak District National Park.

The most visible example of this is the Hope Valley Cement Works where cement is made from limestone and shale quarried in the region. Shale is the underlying rock in many parts of the Peak District. It is most conspicuous at Mam Tor, famous for its exposed cliff-face and frequent landslips. Although the scenery here may look like a man-made quarry, it is in fact the result of natural erosion of the fragile substrate by the elements.

Upper: Hope Valley cement works
Lower: Mam Tor — site of a major landslip

 **Marsh Thistle** *Cirsium palustre*

Despite its common name, marsh thistle is not restricted to marshy habitats and occurs in addition in damp grassy places of all kinds. It is a robust plant, sometimes exceeding 1m in height; the top half of the plant is usually much branched. The spines with which the stems and leaves are armoured provide an excellent defence against grazing animals which, not surprisingly, leave it well alone. The purple flower heads are carried in dense clusters at the ends of the stems. Marsh thistle is common in the Peak District, doing particularly well on neutral soils.

138 **Carline Thistle** *Carlina vulgaris*

Rather unusually, carline thistle resembles a dried, dead head even when it is in flower although this is not to say it is an unattractive plant. Its most distinctive feature is, of course, its flower heads. These may be 30-40mm across and comprise golden-brown disc florets in the centre, surrounded by slender, pointed bracts which are spreading. The leaves are ovate and slender with wavy margins; both leaves and stem are covered in fierce spines. Carline thistle flowers from July to September, but the flower heads retain their appearance long after flowering has finished. It is a plant of limestone grassland.

139 **Musk Thistle** *Carduus nutans*

The drooping flower heads of this attractive plant give rise to its alternative name of nodding thistle. It is a plant that prefers dry areas and often base-rich soils; in the Peak District it is mostly associated with limestone grassland and scrub. Musk thistle is a branched biennial with stems which are winged and armoured with spines; these bear spiny leaves which are pinnately lobed. The nodding flower heads appear between May and August and are up to 50mm across. They comprise densely packed reddish-purple florets.

140 Greater Knapweed *Centaurea scabiosa*
The attractive flower heads of greater knapweed would be
showy enough to grace any cottage garden. The plant can
grow to a height of 90cm and is usually branched to a greater
or lesser degree. The basal leaves are large and pinnately
lobed, with toothed margins; they are borne on stems while
the smaller stem leaves are stalkless. The flower heads may
be 50mm across and comprise reddish-purple florets; the
inner ones are relatively small and compact while the outer
ones are long, deeply divided and spreading. Greater
knapweed is a plant of limestone grassland and flowers from
June to August.

141 Common Knapweed *Centaurea nigra*
The tough, swollen base to the flower heads of this plant
gives rise to its other common name of hardheads. Common
knapweed is a common grassland plant that often grows to a
height of 90cm or more. The leaves are lanceolate and lobed,
the lower ones being larger than the stem leaves. The tall
stalks are sometimes divided near the top and carry the
terminal flower heads. These are 20-30mm across and
comprise reddish-purple florets of uniform size and which do
not spread much. Common knapweed flowers from June to
September and is found in grassy places of all sorts in the
Peak District.

142 Bog Asphodel *Narthecium ossifragum*
Waterlogged, peaty moorland soils and boggy flushes provide
ideal habitats for bog asphodel. This distinctive plant
produces upright spikes of bright yellow flowers that are
showy enough to be seen from a distance, especially if
numerous plants are growing together. The individual flowers
comprise six segments which are arranged in the shape of a
star. After the flowers have finished, and died back, the entire
spike dries orange-red and persists. Bog asphodel has narrow
leaves that grow from the base. The plant is locally common
in the Peak District.

143 Ramsons
Allium ursinum
Walk through a woodland
with ramsons growing on
the ground and you will
soon know it, as a strong
smell of garlic begins to
pervade the air. The plant
sometimes covers large
areas if conditions suit it:
ramsons thrives best in
damp woodlands where the
underlying soil is lime-rich.
Oval, pointed leaves, up to
20cm long, grow from the
base in clumps. From the
centre of these arise a
number of flower stalks
which can be 20cm tall.
These carry almost
spherical loose heads of
white flowers, each one of
which is rather star-
shaped. Ramsons flowers
from April to June and is
very locally common in
the Peak District.

This plant is also known as cuckoo-pint, perhaps because it appears in early May, roughly when cuckoos arrive and begin singing. Groups of arrow-shaped basal leaves can be seen in hedgerows and woodlands in early spring; the upper surface is sometimes dark-spotted. During April and May, an upright stalk is produced, bearing a broad, hooded structure called the spathe. Inside this is a brownish, club-shaped spadix. Later in the year, spikes of red berries develop after the leaves have died back. Lords-and-ladies is locally common in the Peak District.

146 Frog Orchid
Coeloglossum viride
Seen through a hand lens, the flowers of this unusually named plant could fancifully be thought to resemble miniature leaping frogs. The plant has broad, lanceolate leaves at the base but these become smaller and narrower up the stem. In some specimens the flowering spike can be 20cm tall but it is generally much smaller. A spike of 10 to 20

144 Bluebell *Hyacinthoides non-scripta*
Carpets of bluebells are very much a feature of many Peak District woodlands in the spring. Where conditions suit it, the plant grows in profusion and almost to the exclusion of other species. It ideally likes open, airy woodlands where there is plenty of light available from late winter until early summer. Bluebell has an underground bulb from which a spray of linear, basal leaves are produced. The bluish-purple flowers are carried in an inflorescence and are pleasantly scented. Bluebell flowers from April to June.

flowers is carried at the top, these opening from the bottom upwards. The individual flowers are greenish but often marked with reddish-brown; they comprise a divided lower lip and a hooded upper lip. In the Peak District, it grows on limestone grassland.

147 Burnt Orchid *Orchis ustulata*
The tiny burnt orchid is one of Britain's most attractive species but it needs close scrutiny to do it justice. The flower spikes are relatively dense and rather uniformly cylindrical. The open flowers, which occur lower down the spike, are white with red markings while, in contrast, the unopen flowers at the top are dark red; the whole effect is one of a burnt tip. Burnt orchid is a plant of limestone grassland in the Peak District. It flowers during May and June, with some populations flowering in July, and is rather local.

148 Early Purple Orchid *Orchis mascula*
From February onwards, a walk through a Peak District woodland may reveal the dark-spotted leaf rosettes of early purple orchids. In undisturbed areas of native woodland, the plant can become fairly common. It produces sometimes tall spikes of flowers from April to June, roughly when bluebells are also in bloom. The spikes of flowers are usually rather loose with individual flowers being pinkish-purple in colour. Early purple orchids will sometimes grow in grassland as well as woodland but do not generally thrive where the underlying soil is acid.

149 Pyramidal Orchid *Anacamptis pyramidalis*
Among the Peak District's orchid species, the pyramidal is one of the few that can be identified by name alone. In the summer months, generally from June to August, the plant produces dense conical spikes of flowers, which alternatively could be described as pyramidal in shape. Individual flowers

are deep pink in colour with a three-lobed lower lip and a long spur; the leaves are lanceolate and whitish green. Pyramidal orchid is primarily a plant of limestone grassland and is very locally common in suitable habitats in the region.

150 Common Spotted Orchid *Dactylorhiza fuchsii*
Growing in grassland and scrub, and sometimes even on roadside verges, the common spotted orchid is one of the most familiar of its kind in Britain. It has broad, dark green basal leaves that are usually spotted with dark purple; these appear as a rosette long before the flower spike and flowers are produced. The flower stalk can be 50cm or more tall and it carries a long spike of flowers. These are usually pink and, when viewed closely, are marked with dark purple and have a three-lobed lower lip. Common spotted orchid is locally common on neutral to lime-rich soils in the Peak District.

145

148

149

150

NON-FLOWERING PLANTS

151 Bracken *Pteridium aquilinum*
Bracken is an amazingly resilient and widespread fern in
Britain. In the Peak District, it thrives best in moorland
settings and in woodlands, especially of oak, on neutral to
acid soils. The first sign of new growth comes in the spring
when young curled fronds, covered in brown scales, push
through the soil. These soon unfurl and the fronds expand,
becoming bright green; in the autumn, they turn golden-brown
and persist until heavy rains and frost in late autumn and
winter finally destroy their remains. Bracken is locally very
common in the region.

152 Lemon-scented Fern *Thelypteris limbosperma*
This species' alternative name of mountain fern gives a clue
as to its preferred habitat: lemon-scented fern grows most
characteristically on upland slopes in moorland regions. The
fronds grow in tufts or clumps from a basal point and, in
suitable habitats, the tufts grow side by side forming large
patches. Compared to bracken or many other ferns, the
fronds are a fresh green colour and, when crushed, give off
the strong lemon scent that gives rise to the commonly used
'English name. Lemon-scented fern is locally common in the
Peak District.

153 Beech Fern *Thelypteris phegopteris*
Other than a passing resemblance between the colour of
beech fern fronds and that of fresh beech leaves, this species
has no particular association with its namesake tree; it is
seldom found growing with beech nor is there any similarity in
the shapes of the fern fronds and the tree leaves. It grows in
damp woodlands and among shaded rocks in the Peak
District. The fronds can reach a length of 15cm or so and are
roughly triangular in outline; characteristically the fronds are
carried horizontally from an almost upright stalk.

154 Wall Rue *Asplenium ruta-muraria*
The intricate fronds of wall rue do bear more than a passing
resemblance to the leaves of rue and the plant does indeed
often grow on walls; damp, shady rocks and bridges offer
alternative sites in the Peak District. The stalked fronds are
highly branched, the tips appearing as triangular-shaped
blades. In many situations, the fronds arising from a single
plant overlap considerably and are not held in one plane; the
result is a complex, interwoven mass. Groups of plants
sometimes follow the gaps between stones in drystone walls.

155 Maidenhair Spleenwort *Asplenium trichomanes*
Damp rock faces with trickling water or shady stone walls are
ideal sites for maidenhair spleenwort to flourish. Fronds of this
attractive little fern can be up to 10cm long. They comprise a
blackish central stalk on which 25 to 30 opposite pairs of
leaflets are carried; these are largest at the base and narrow
towards the tip. The leaflets gradually fall off during their
second year but the wiry stalks remain alongside the new
growth of fronds. Maidenhair spleenwort is locally common in
the Peak District, despite its restricted choice of habitat.

FISH

*Being a mainly upland region
with fast-flowing rivers and streams,
the fish fauna of the Peak District
is especially varied when compared
to lowland regions of Britain.*

The streams and rivers do, however,
harbour characteristic species such as
brown trout, bullheads and brook
lampreys, while grayling can be found in
more tranquil waters. Many of the
reservoirs, such as Ladybower, have been
stocked with fish for anglers, the main
interest coming from brown trout.

*Upper: Immature Brown Trout Salmo trutta fario
Lower: Brook Lamprey Lampetra planeri*

PLACES OF INTEREST

This is just a selection of the many places to visit in the Peak District. For further information, contact the Peak Park Joint Planning Board at Bakewell (see opposite).

• Castleton Show Caverns

There are three spectacular caverns here:

Blue John — where the famous Blue Johnstone is mined.
Open all year daily.

Peak — with an underground walk of nearly 0.5 mile.
Open Easter to end October daily.

Speedwell — with a mile-long boat trip.
Open all year daily.

• Chatsworth House

Chatsworth, near Bakewell.
Tel: 01246 582204

Magnificent home of the Duke and Duchess of Devonshire. Fine parkland plus many other attractions and seasonal events.
Open March to November daily.

• Haddon Hall

Tel: 01629 812855

A fascinating house that has scarcely changed in the last 400 years. Owned by the National Trust.
Open April to September.

• Lea Gardens

Tel: 01629 534380

Woodland gardens covering over 3 acres with rhododendrons, azaleas and rock plants.
Open March to July daily.

• National Tramway Museum

Matlock Road, Crich.
Tel: 01773 852565

Tramcars of all kinds exhibited in a former quarry. Exhibitions, displays and tram rides.
Open March to November at weekends and on certain other days.

• Riber Castle Wildlife Park

Tel: 01629 582073

Rare breeds and endangered species of birds and animals in 20 acres.
Open daily all year, except Christmas Day.

USEFUL ADDRESSES

Countryside Commission
John Dower House
Crescent Place
Cheltenham, Glos GL50 3RA

Derbyshire County Council
County Offices
Matlock, Derbys DE4 3AG

Derbyshire Wildlife Trust
Elvaston Country Park
Derbys DE7 3EP

English Nature (Headquarters)
Northminster House
Peterborough PE1 1VA

National Trust (Regional Office)
Clumber Park Stableyard
Worksop, Notts S80 3BE

Peak Park Joint Planning Board
Aldern House
Baslow Road, Bakewell, Derbys DE4 1AE

RSPB (Headquarters)
The Lodge
Sandy, Beds SG19 2DL.

Wildfowl Trust
Slimbridge, Glos GL2 7BT

Photo credits:
All photographs were supplied by Nature Photographers Ltd and were taken by Paul Sterry with the following exceptions: C. Carver — 2, 18, 25, 29, 41, 47, 54; Paul Knight — 4, P. J. Newman — 5, 12, 13, 14, 20, 34, 38; E. A. Janes — 6, 16, 24, 45, Stone in the Peak District (upper); R. Bush — 7, 119, page 6, page 7 (lower), Lathkill Dale (lower), Monk's Dale (upper), Lead Mining (upper); R. T. Smith — 8; W. S. Paton — 11, 53; K. Carlson — 19; D. Bonsall — 21; F. V. Blackburn — 30, 32; A. K. Davies — 36; D. Smith — 46; A. Cleave — 71, 74, 77, 80, 92, 101, 136, 152, 153, page 7 (upper), Cement and Shale (both), Fish (upper); C. Grey-Wilson — 72; B. Burbidge — 115.

INDEX